TREASURY OF

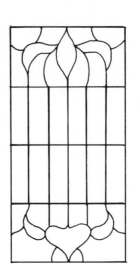

TRADITIONAL

STAINED GLASS DESIGNS

Ann V. Winterbotham

Dover Publications, Inc.
New York

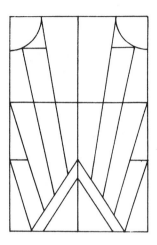

Published in Canada by General Publishing Company, Ltd., 30 Lesmill Road, Don Mills, Toronto, Ontario.
Published in the United Kingdom by Constable and Company, Ltd.

Treasury of Traditional Stained Glass Designs is a new work, first published by Dover Publications, Inc., in 1981.

DOVER *Pictorial Archive* SERIES

International Standard Book Number: 0-486-24084-3
Library of Congress Catalog Card Number: 80-69595

Manufactured in the United States of America
Dover Publications, Inc.
31 East 2nd Street
Mineola, N.Y. 11501

INTRODUCTION

All the designs in this book can be characterized as traditional and domestic; they are all copied from windows in ordinary houses. I have not included any religious or commercial work, or grand ''art'' windows such as those designed by William Morris and other mastercraftsmen of the ''Arts and Crafts Movement.'' Most of my subjects I found in London, because that is where I live; the others are largely from towns in the south of England. Domestic stained glass is not, of course, confined to the South, and I hope eventually to get further afield. I record the designs by the simple if laborious method of walking around every street in a chosen area with pencil and graph paper pad in hand, noting the leading, colors, position and approximate size, redrawing to a standard format later.

On and around front doors is where one usually finds stained glass windows; also on side walls where houses are too close for comfort.

I have found that Victorian windows often have a double border—the outer clear, the inner ruby red or, less commonly, blue. The geometric designs, based on circles, squares and triangles, are of pale tints of subtle colors: olive green, ochre, yellow, amber, pink, mauve and light blue. Flowers, berries and leaves are darker, more primary shades of green and red. Toward the end of the Victorian period and into the Edwardian, more yellows were used, and opaques. Also a larger range of textures or relief patterns in clear glass were employed. Victorian windows were usually all color, whereas the Edwardians liked more light in their rooms and so used much more clear glass, making the contrasting textures rich and sparkling. In late Victorian and Edwardian windows hints of Art Nouveau curves and ovals soften the earlier geometry. Geometric designs appear again in the 1920's and 30's, but these more recent works have more of a diagonal, vertical and horizontal style, with bright clear colors. ''Staining'' or painting was used in all periods sparingly to add detail to representational windows. Victorian windows sometimes have a small round painting of birds or flowers at the center.

My illustrations on the covers of this edition show designs and color schemes characteristic of Victorian (inside back cover), Edwardian (front cover), 1920's (inside front cover) and 1930's (back cover) stained glass windows.

I first became interested in this subject when I was commissioned to do some color drawings for a book and was captivated by the combination of strong line and color in domestic stained glass windows. After doing some designs for myself, I began to learn the craft and so to study the examples around me. As these windows are in ordinary houses, they are gradually disappearing as panels are broken or wooden frames decay. I wanted to record them and to learn from their relative simplicity. Many would have been almost mass-produced, and so represent the maximum variety and effect for the minimum effort. These windows present few technical problems and so I hope will be of interest to students of the craft as well as to architectural historians.

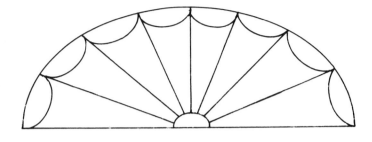

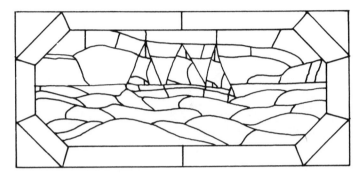

VICTORIAN

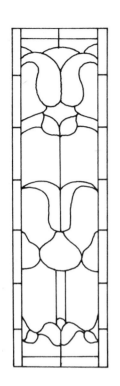
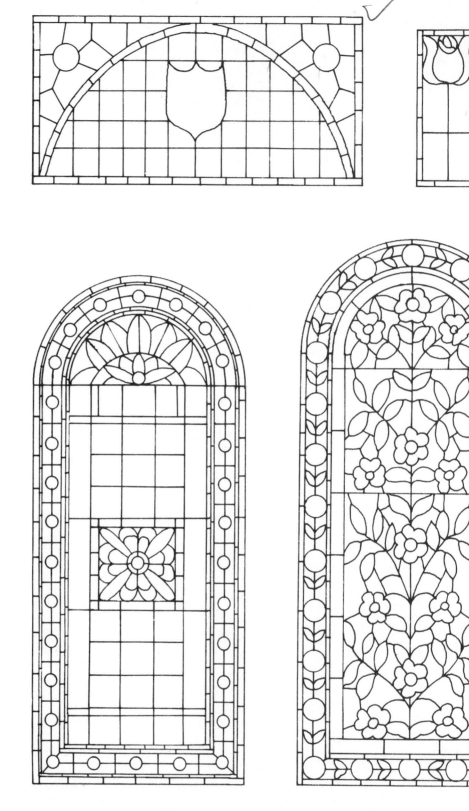
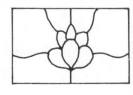

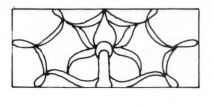

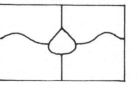

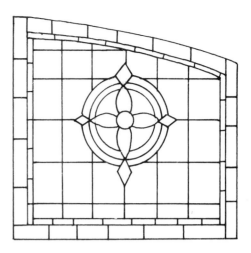

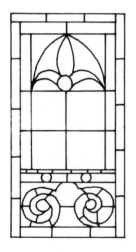

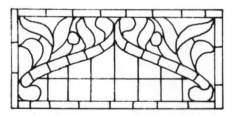

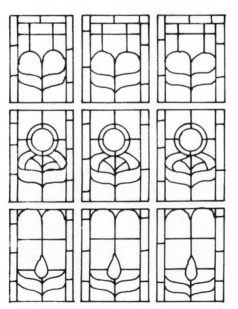

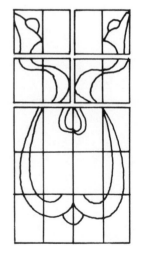

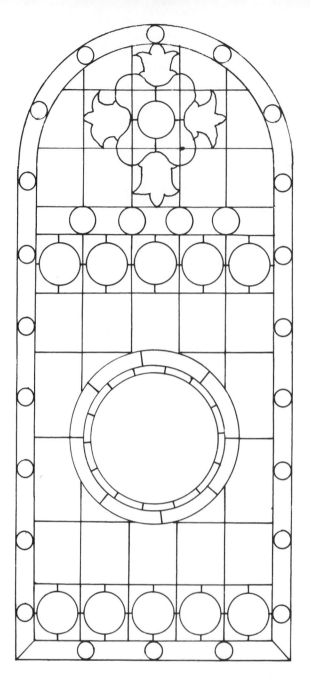
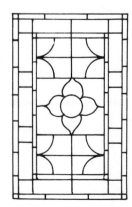

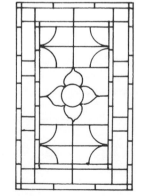

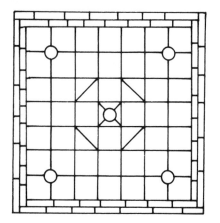

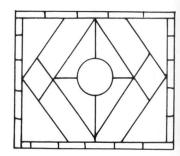

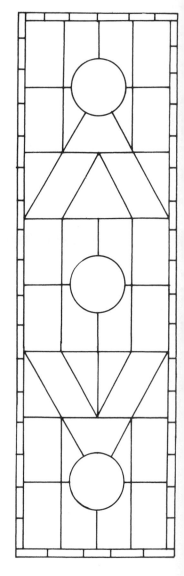
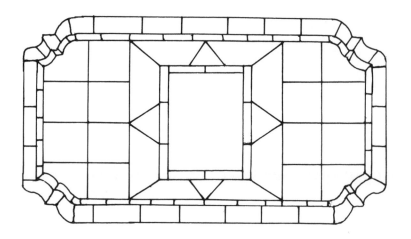
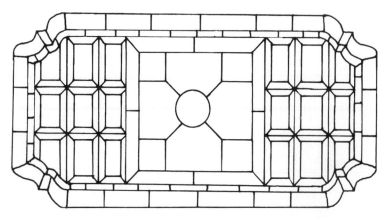
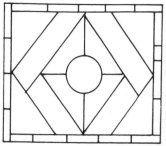

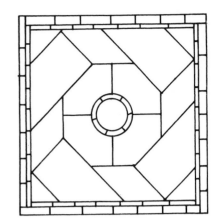

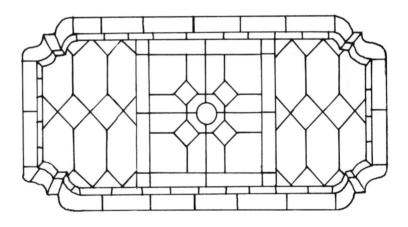

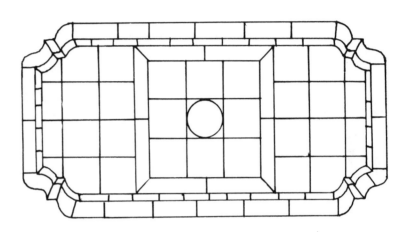
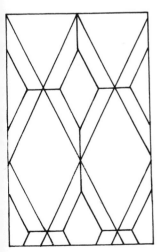
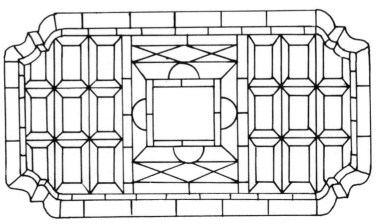

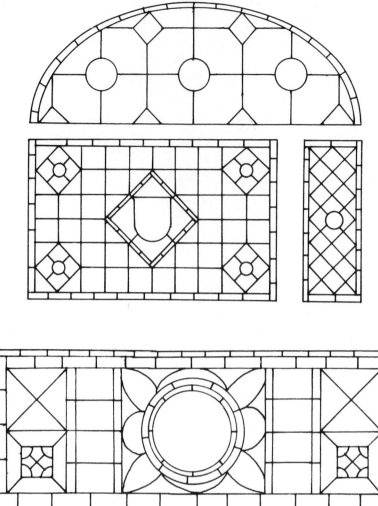
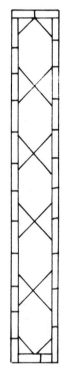

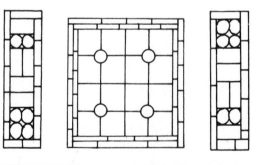
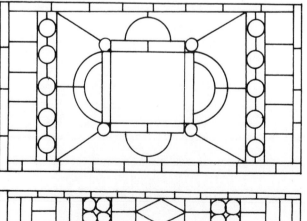

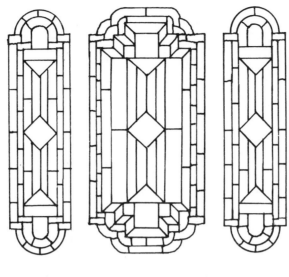

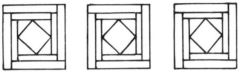

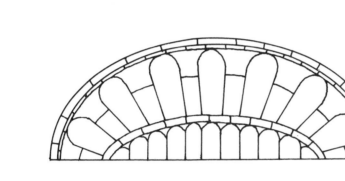

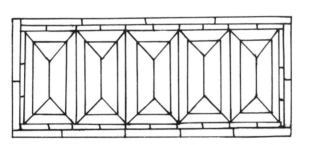

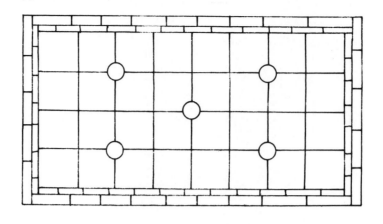

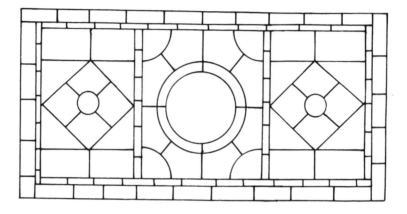

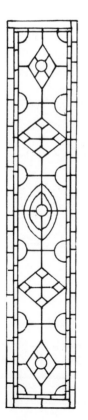

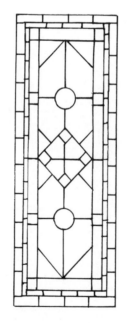

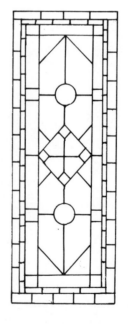

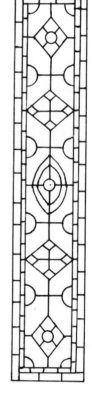

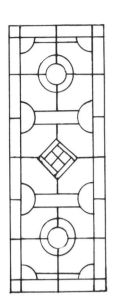
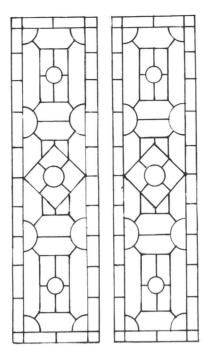
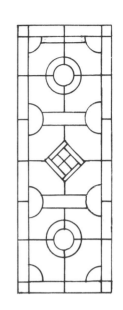
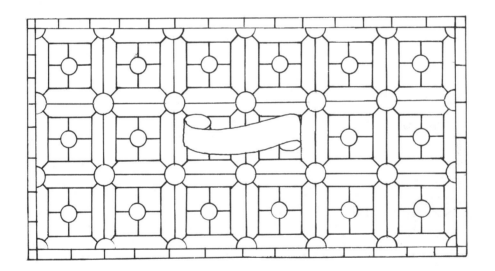
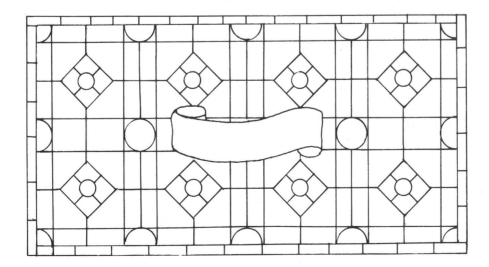

Victorian 13

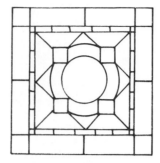

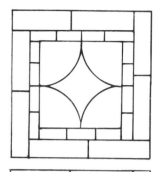

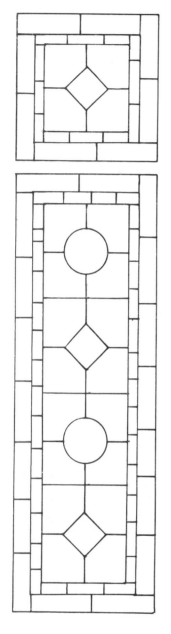

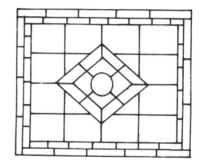

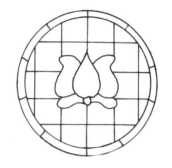

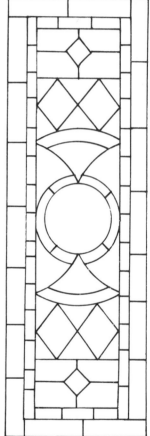

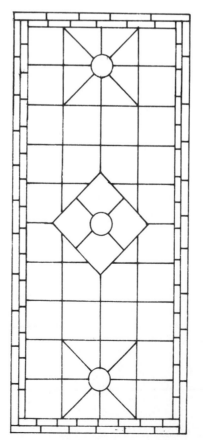

14   *Victorian*

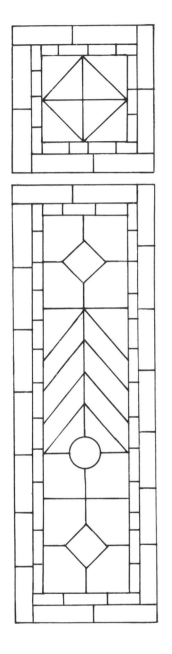

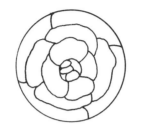

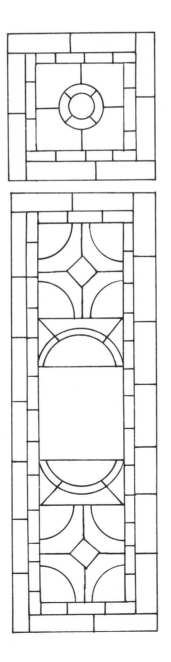

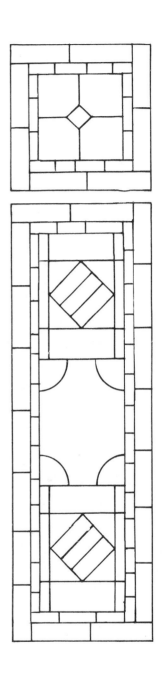

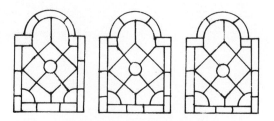

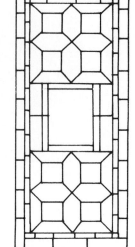

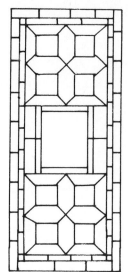

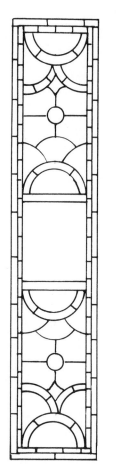

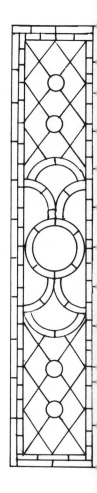

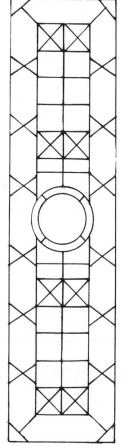

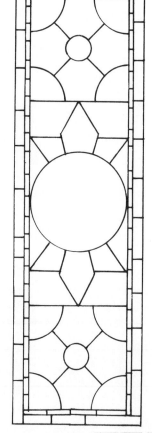

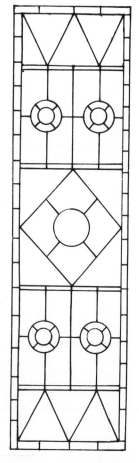

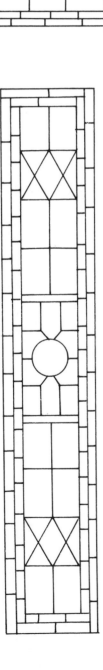
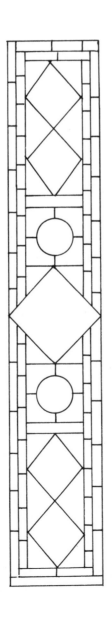
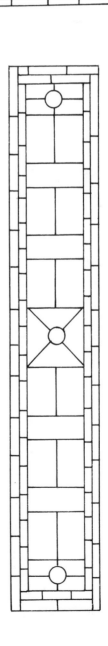
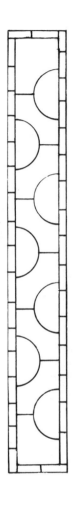

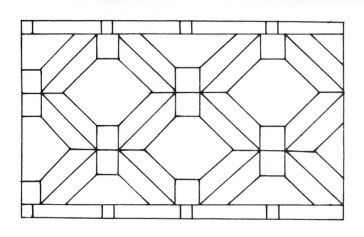

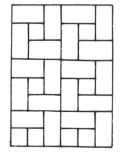

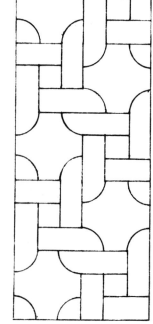

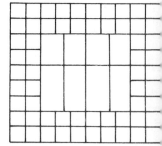

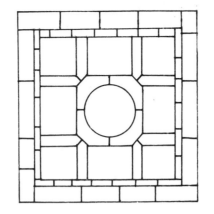

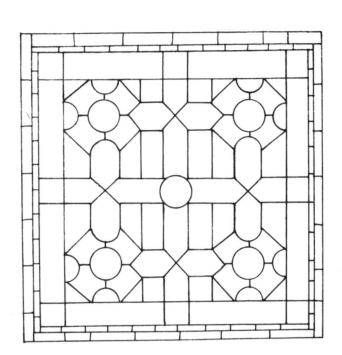

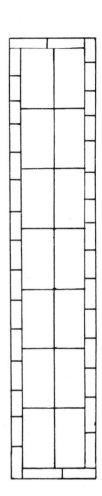

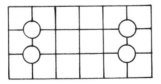

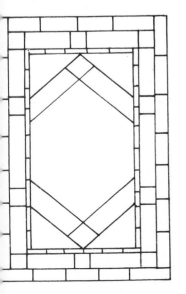

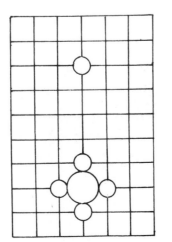

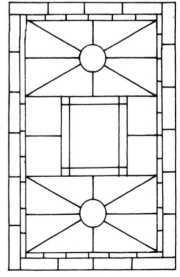

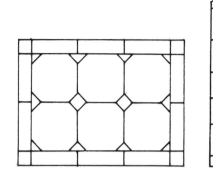
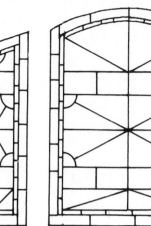
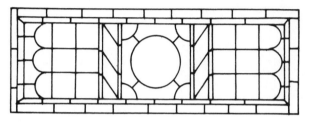
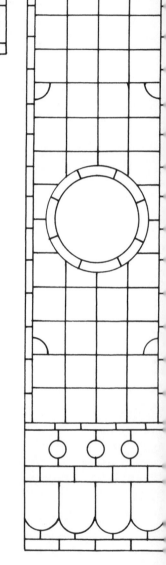
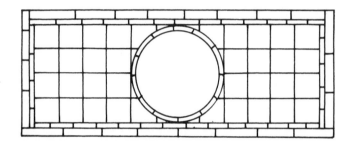
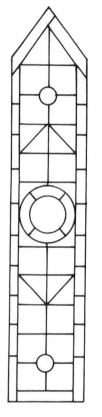
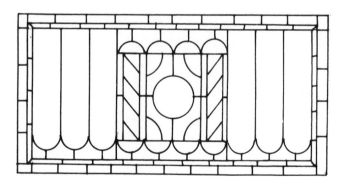
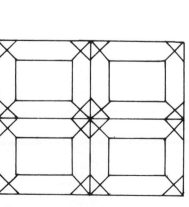
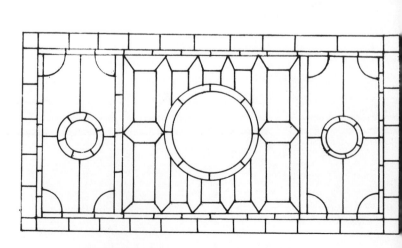

EDWARDIAN

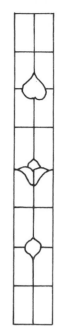

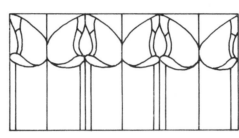

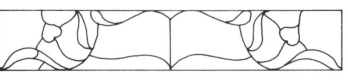

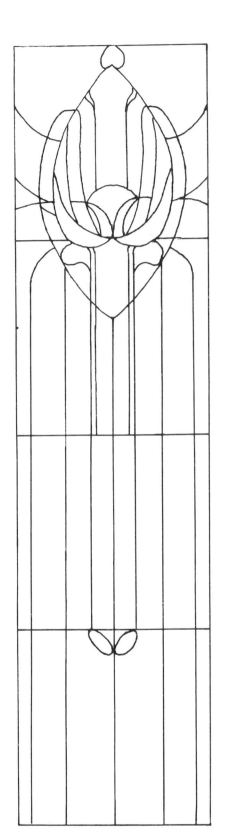

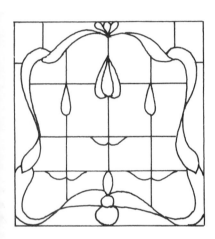

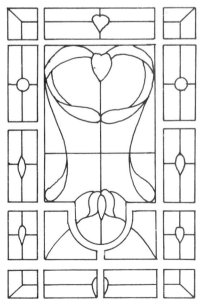

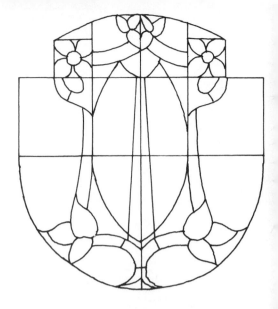

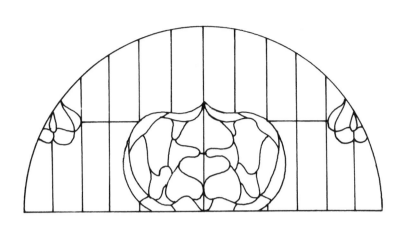

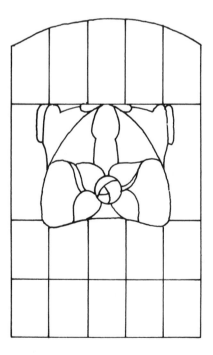

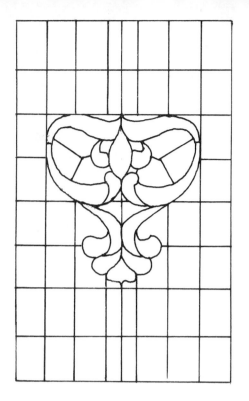
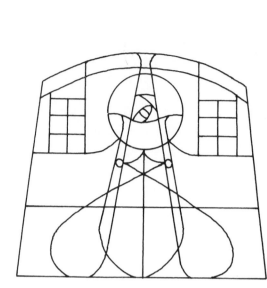
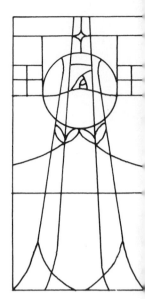
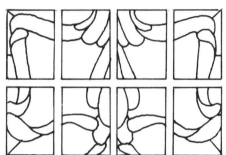
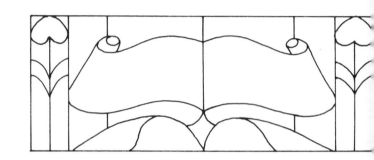
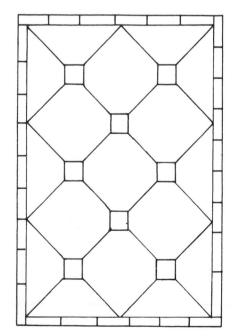
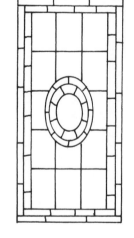
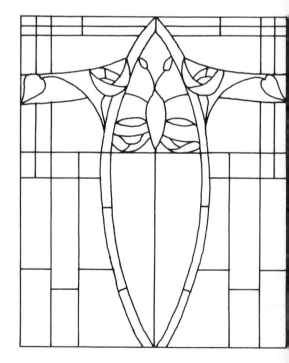

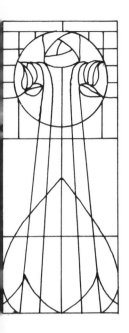
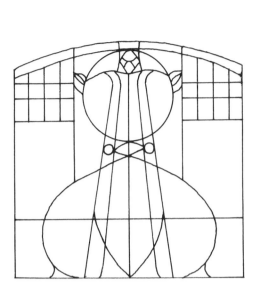

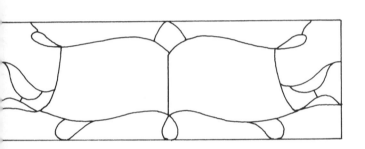
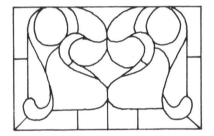
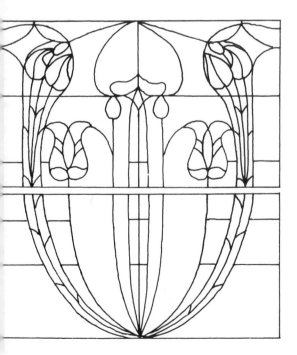
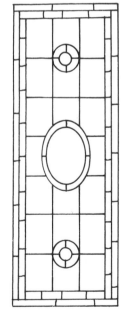
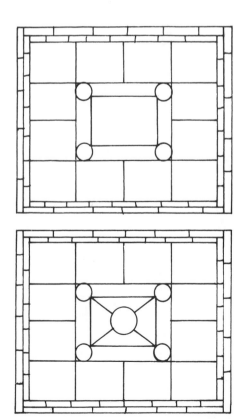

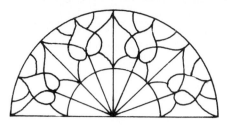

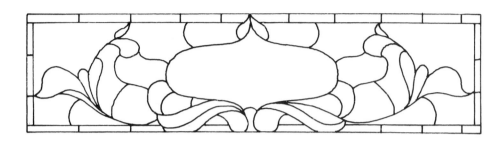

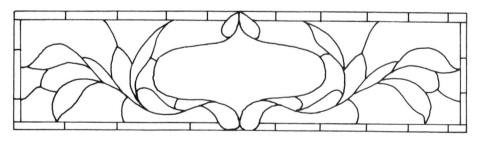

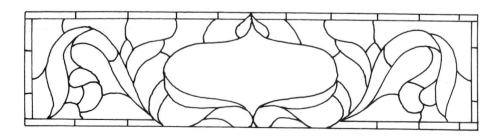

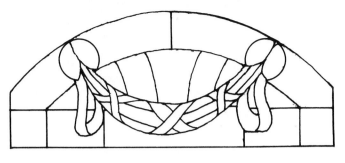
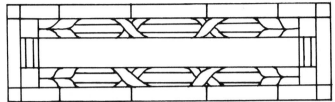
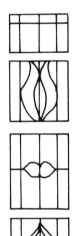

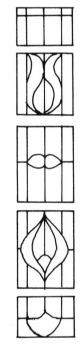

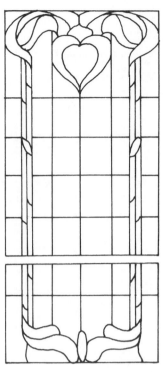

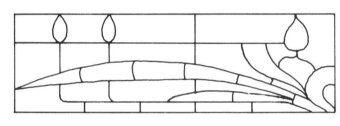

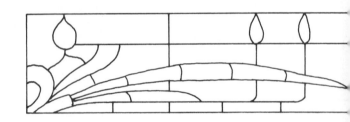

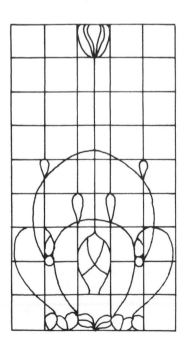

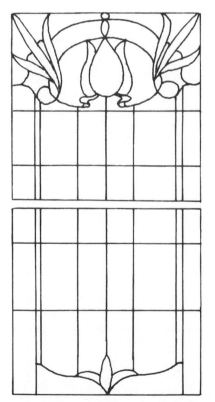

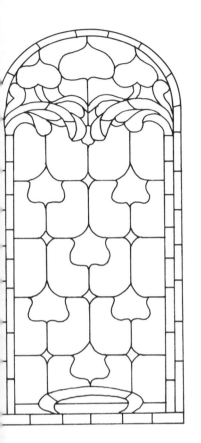
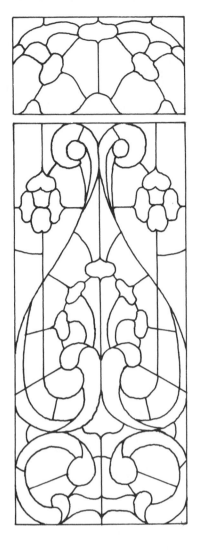

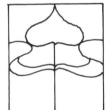
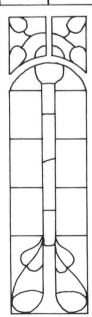

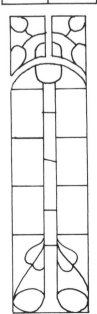

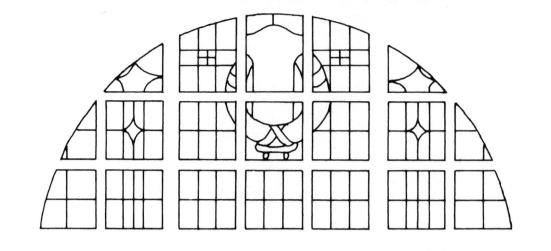

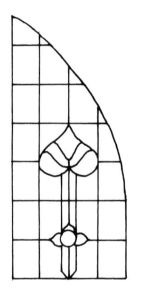

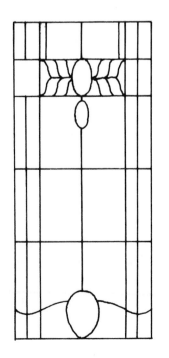

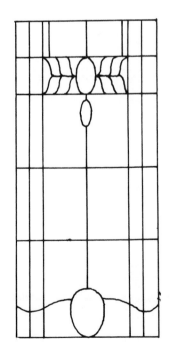

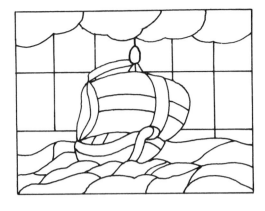

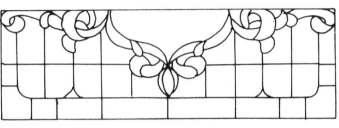

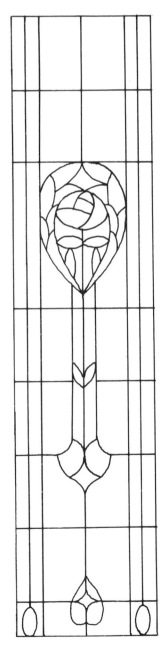

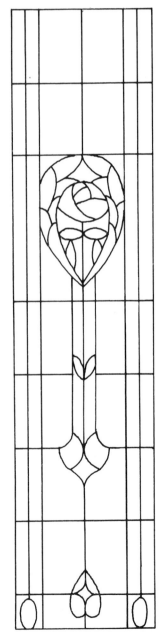

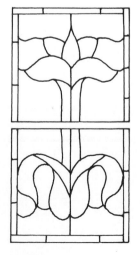

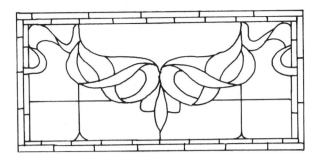

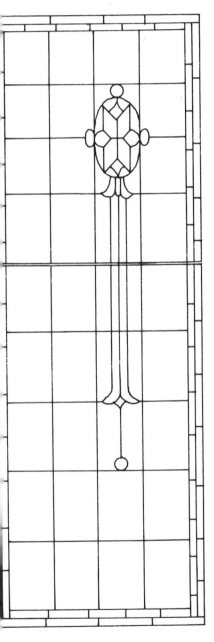

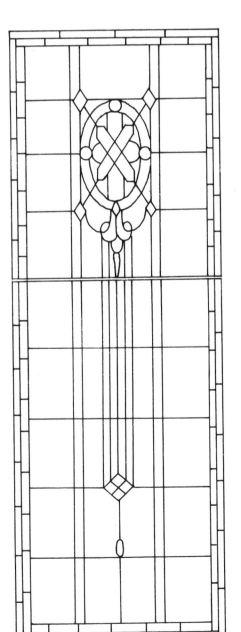

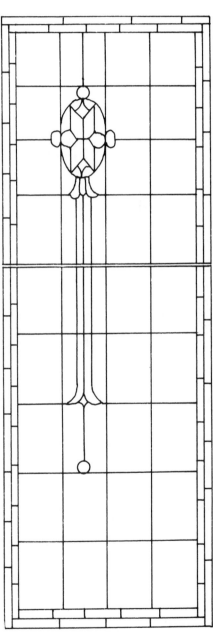

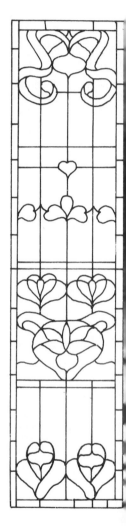

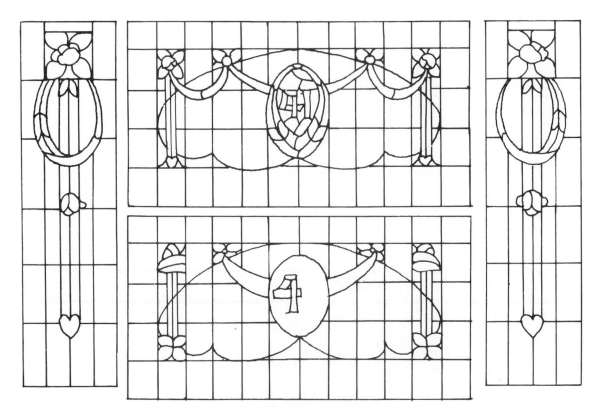

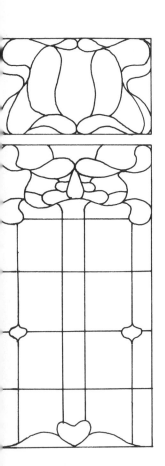

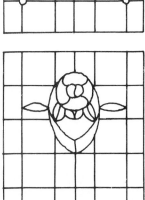

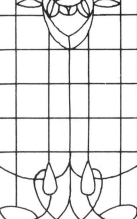

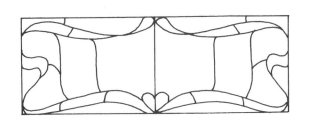

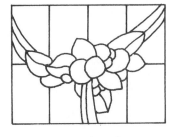

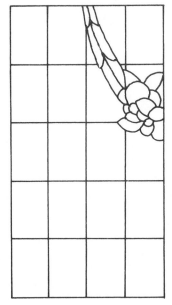

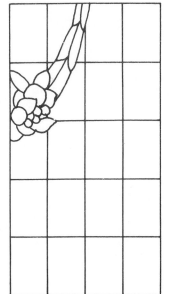

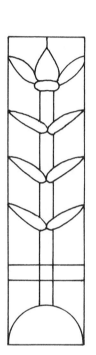

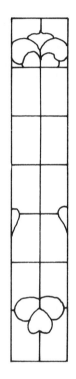

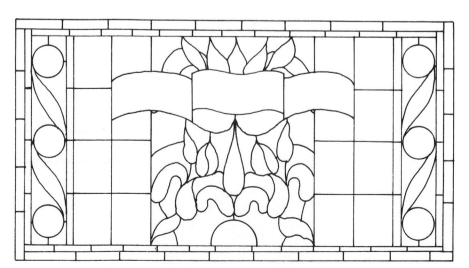

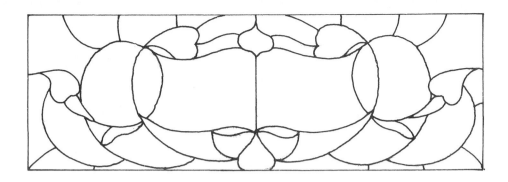

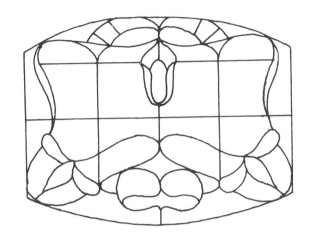

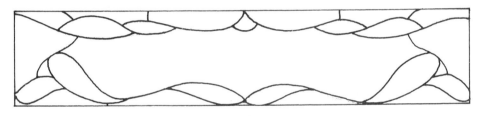

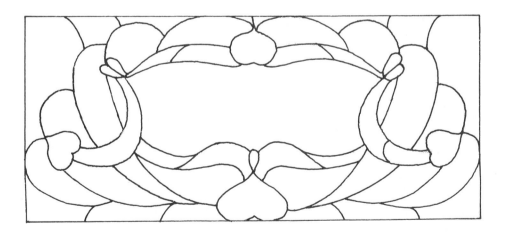

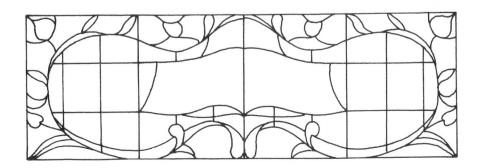

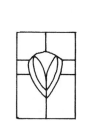
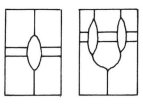
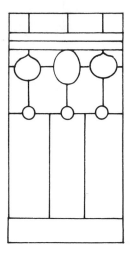
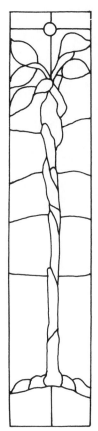
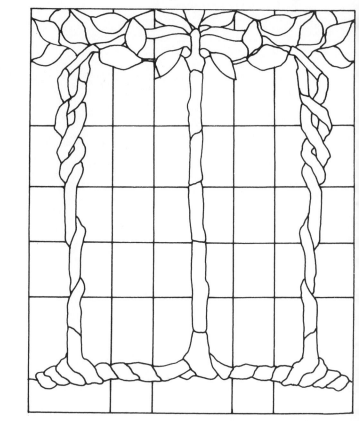
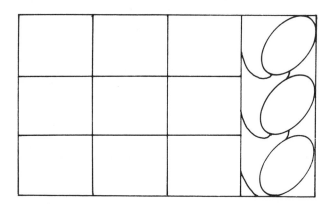
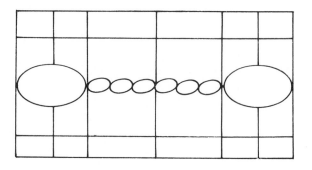
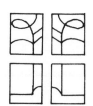
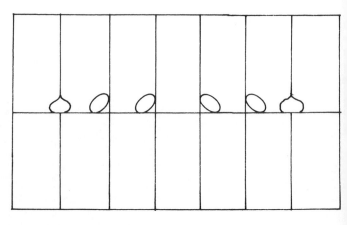

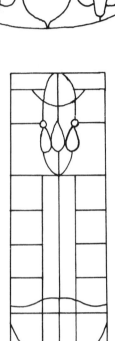

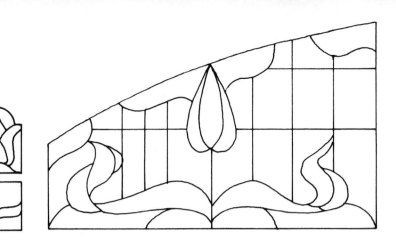

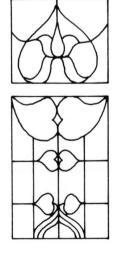
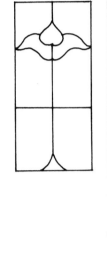
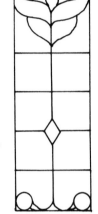
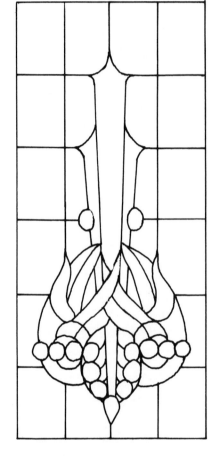
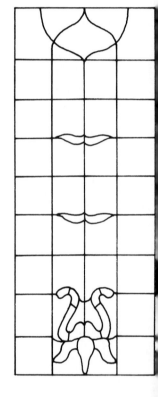
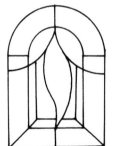

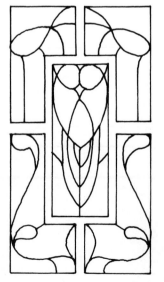
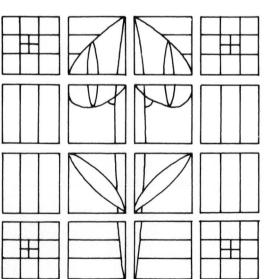
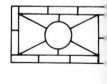

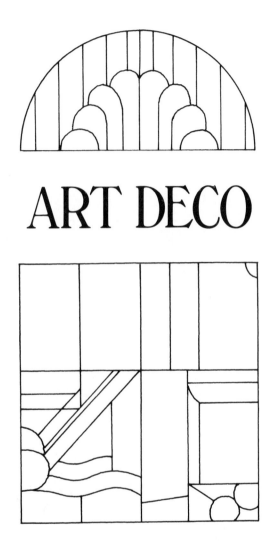

ART DECO

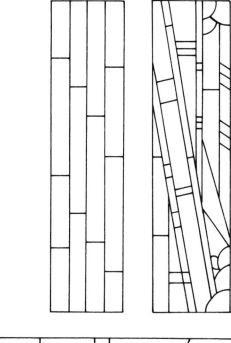

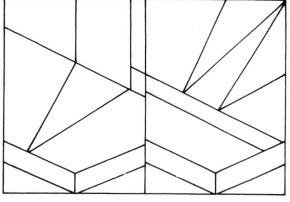

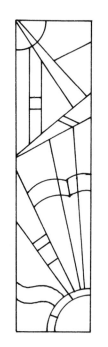

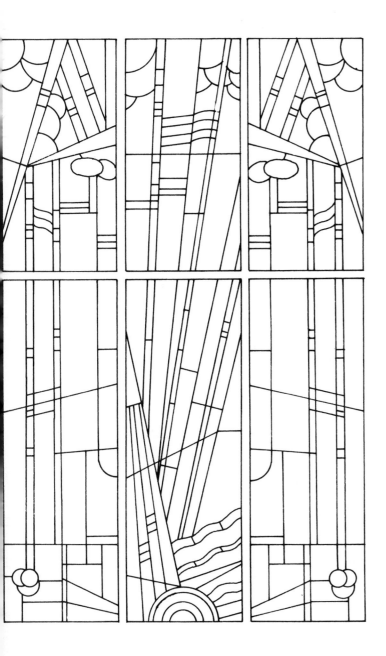

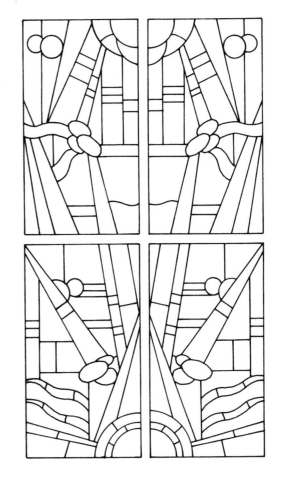

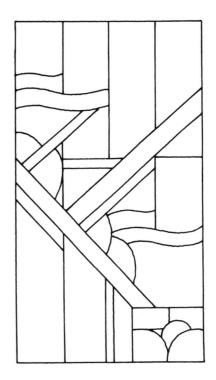

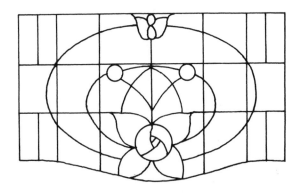

1930's

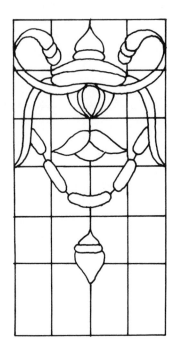

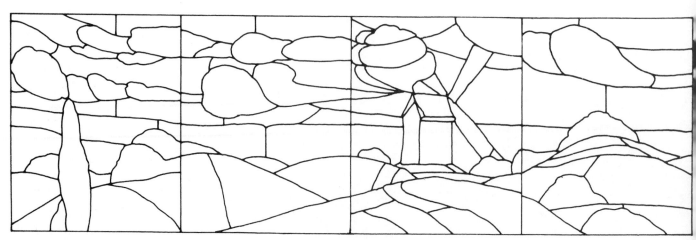

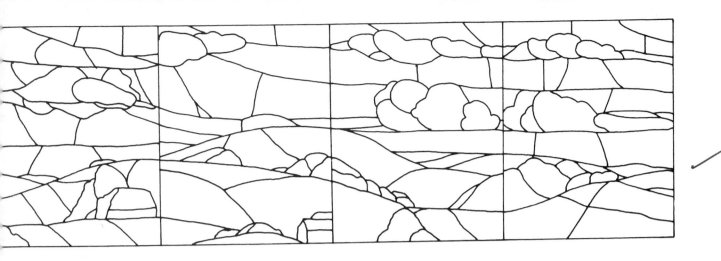

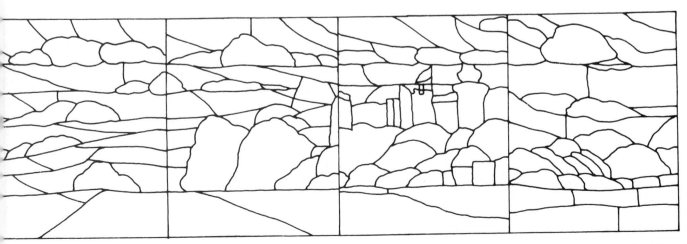

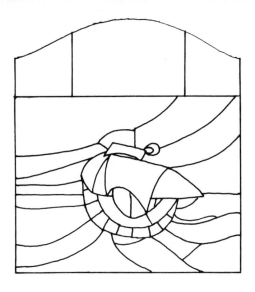

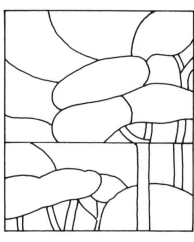

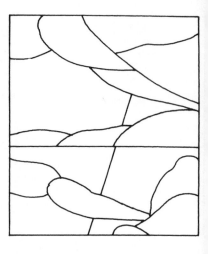

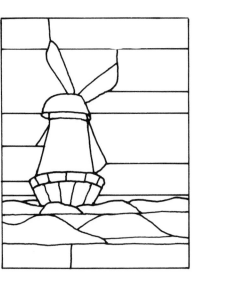

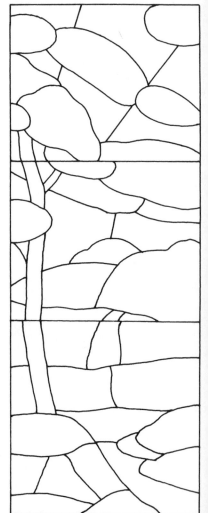

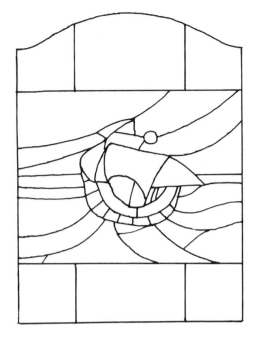

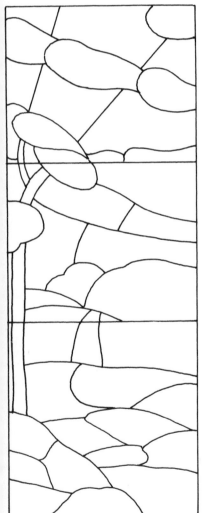

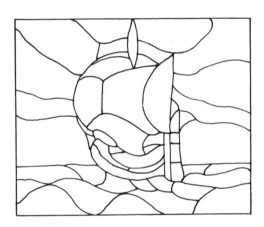

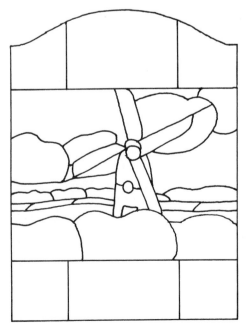

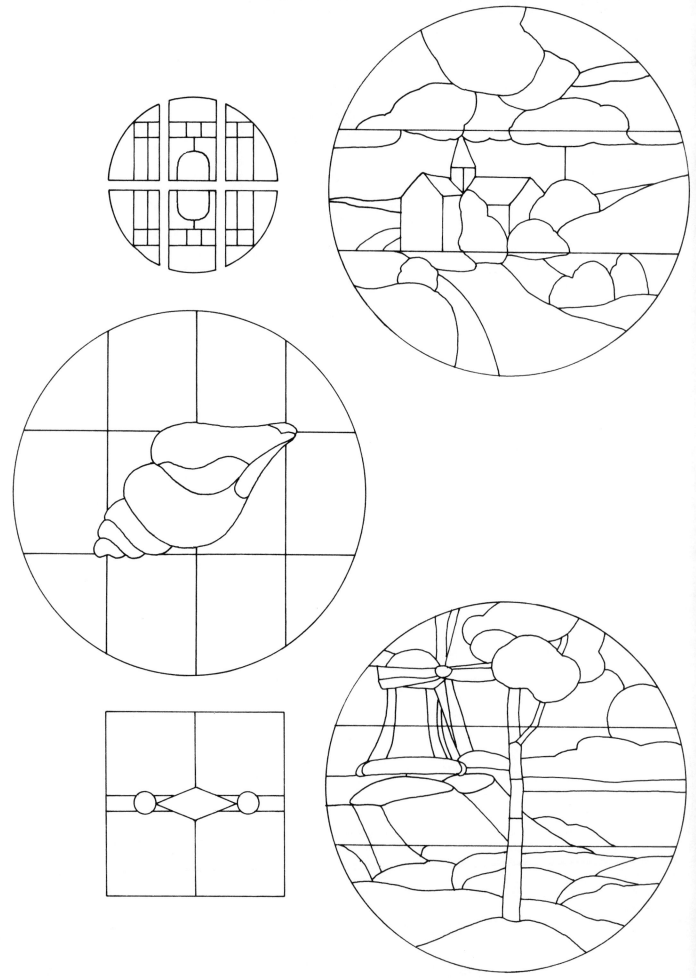

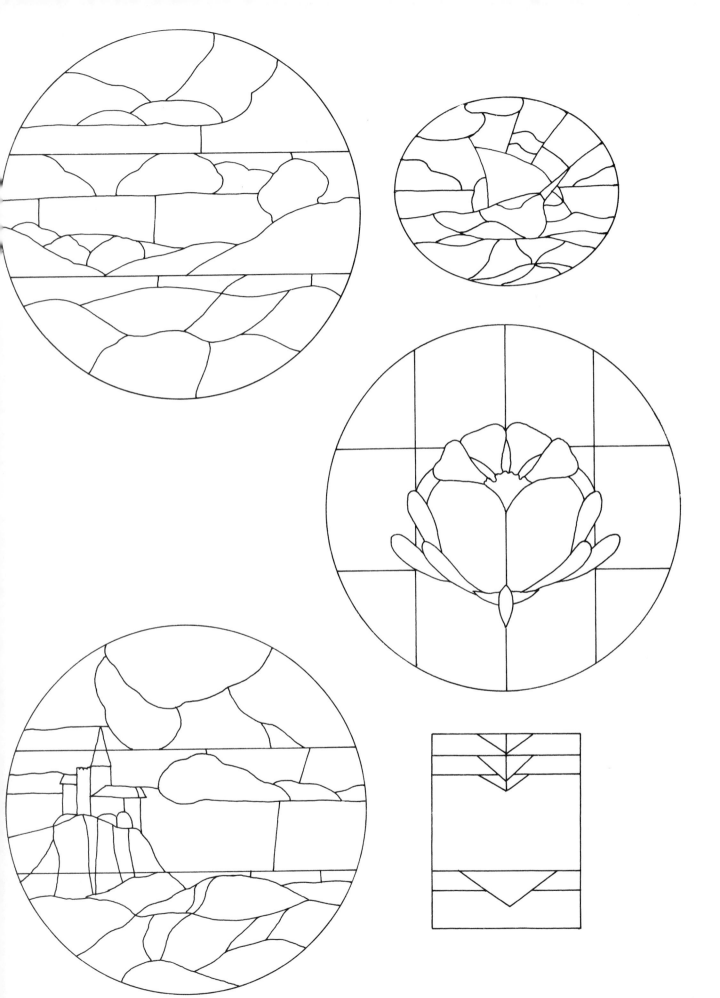

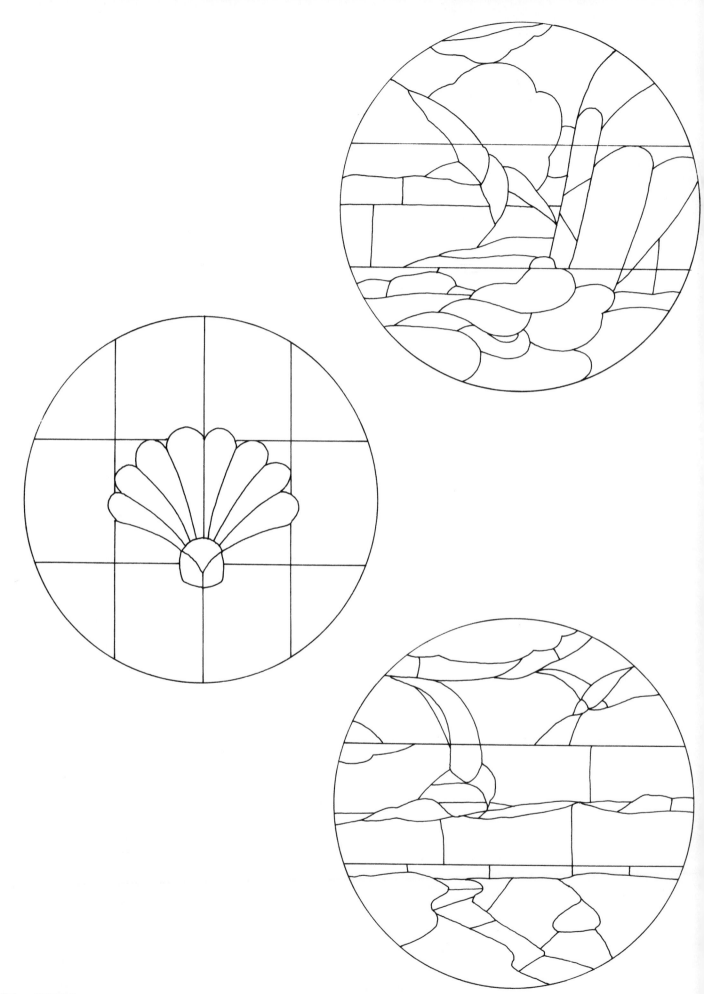

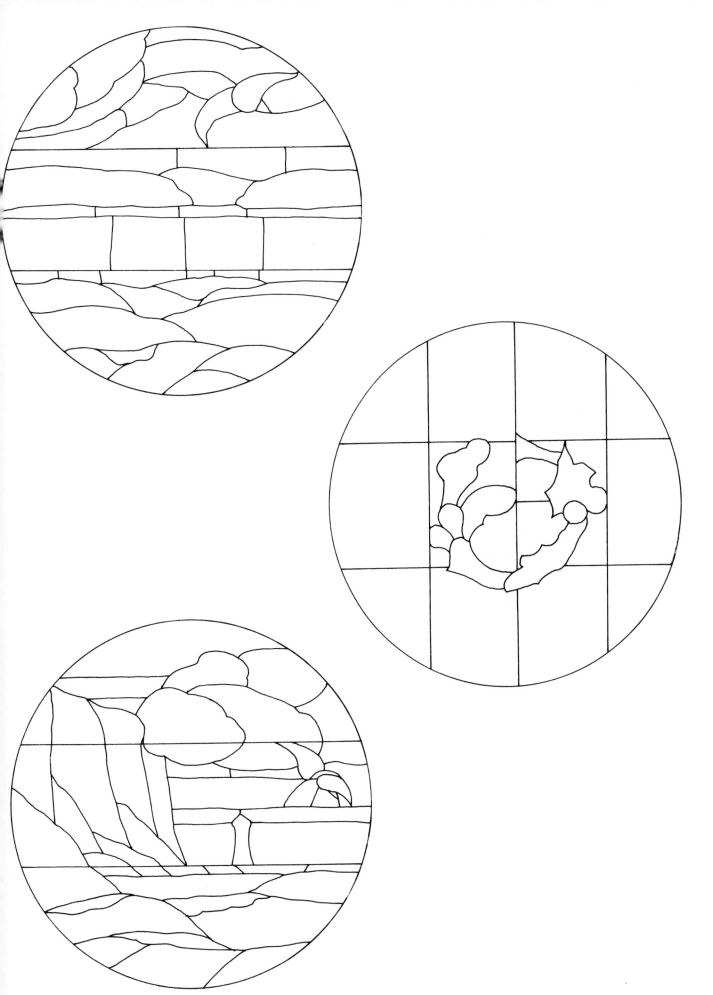

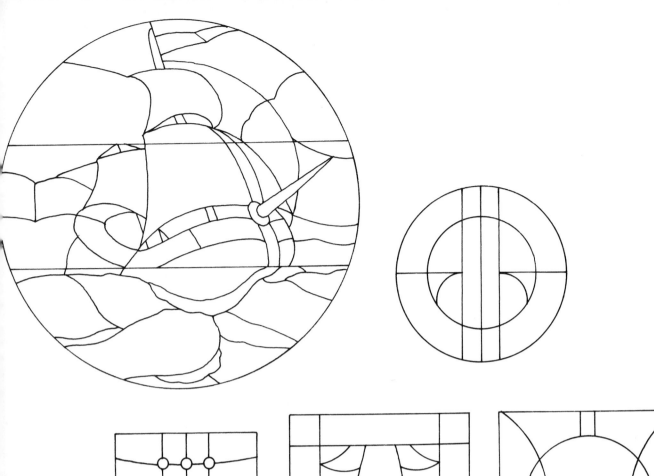

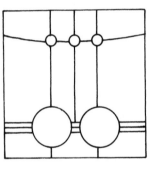

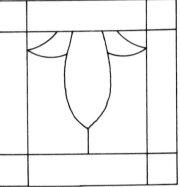

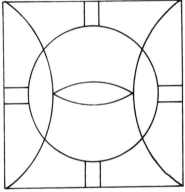

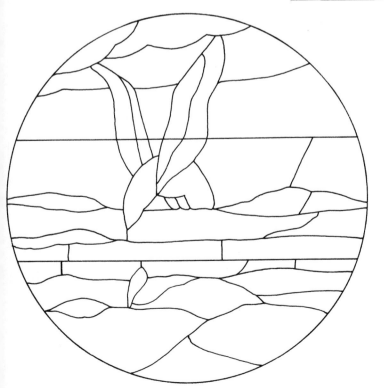

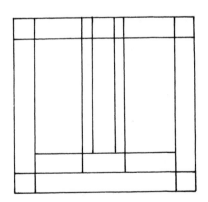

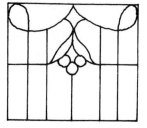

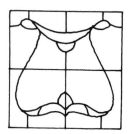
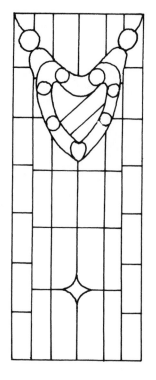

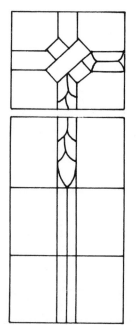
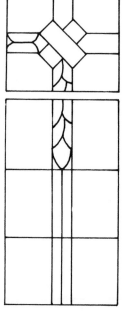
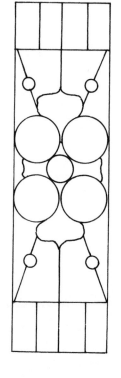
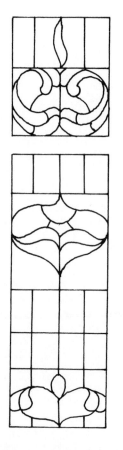
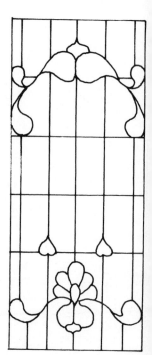

60   *1930's*

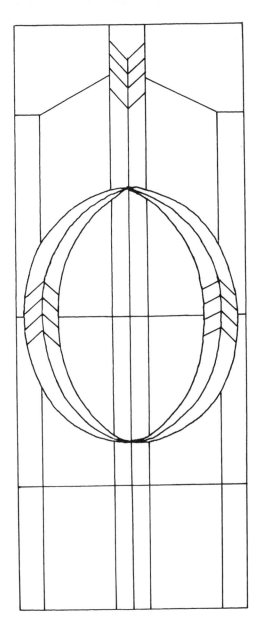

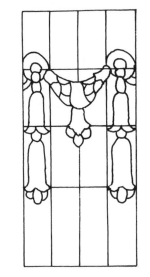

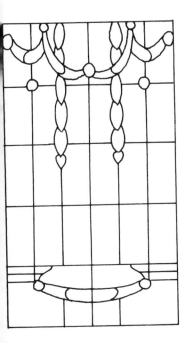

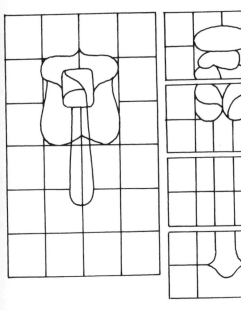

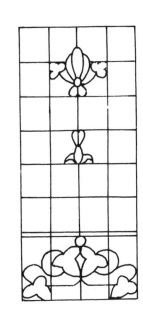

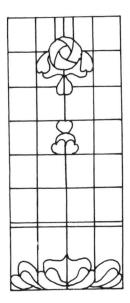

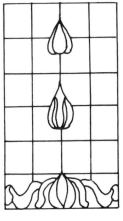

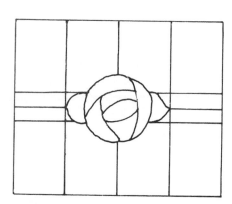

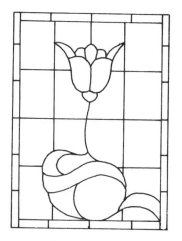

62 *1930's*

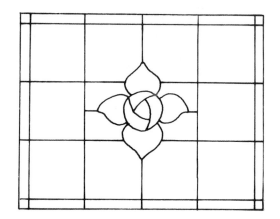

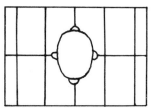
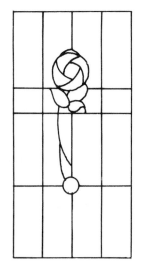
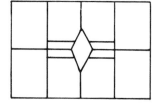
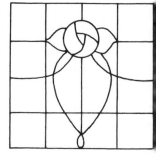

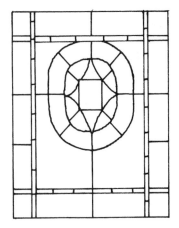
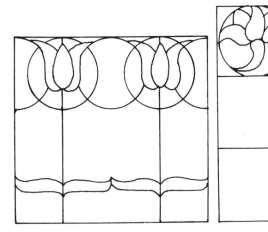
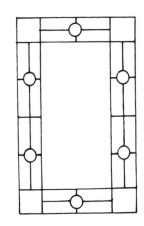

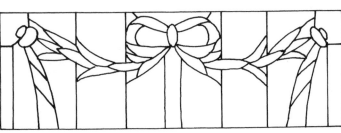

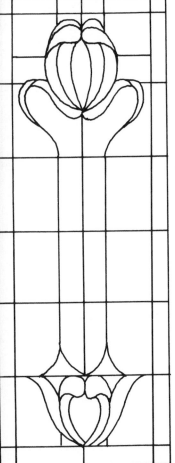
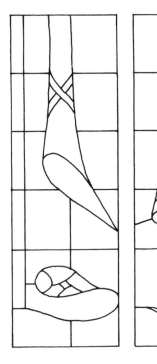

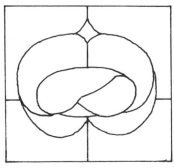

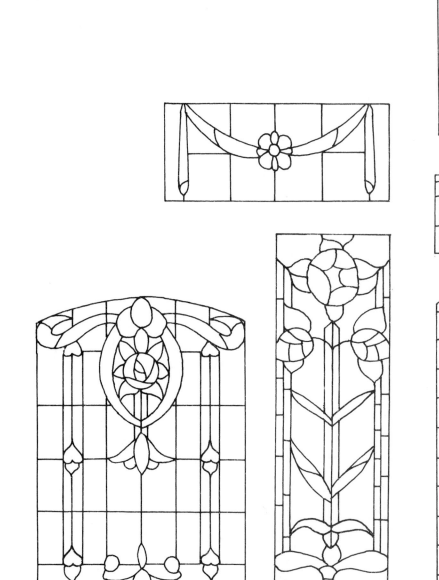

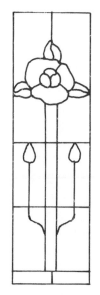

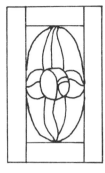
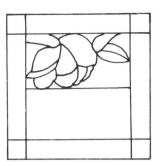
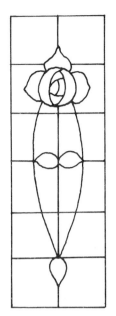
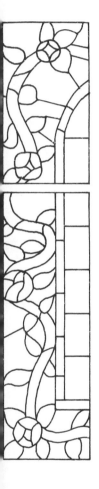
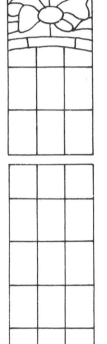
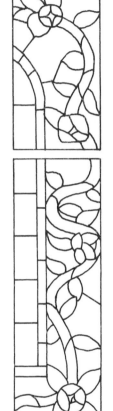

1940's

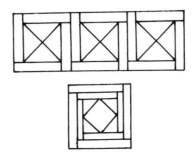

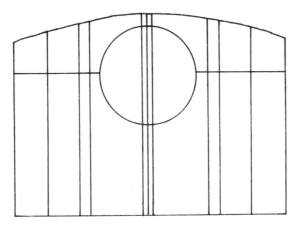

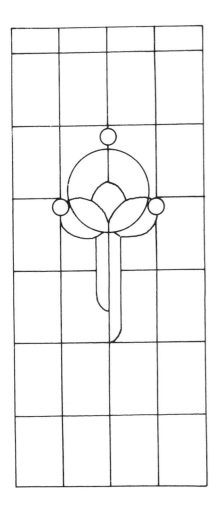
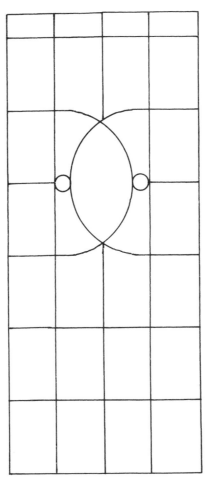
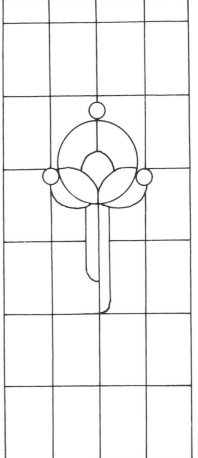

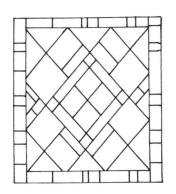
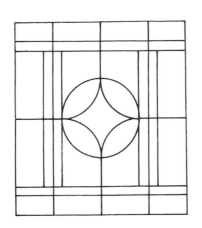
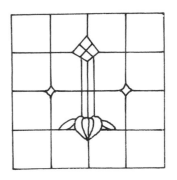

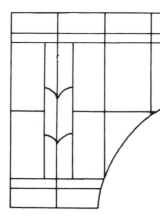

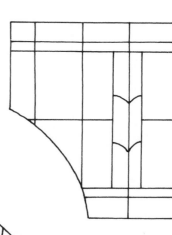

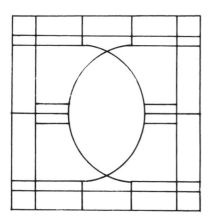

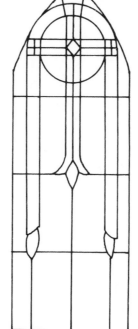

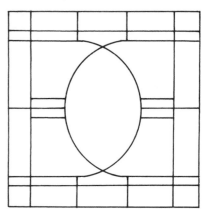

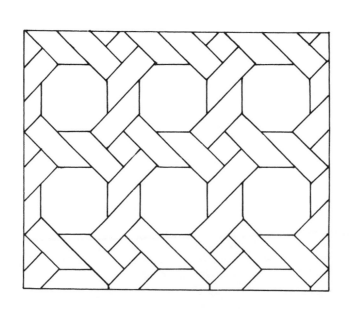

DOVER CRAFT BOOKS